HER OWN *WORST* ENEMY

A Serious Comedy About Choosing a Career

Integrated Skills Through Drama

Her Own Worst Enemy
Alice Savage

Only the Best Intentions (forthcoming)
Alice Savage

Out of Control (forthcoming)
Alice Savage

Other Books by Alphabet Publishing

Successful Group Work—13 Activities to Teach Teamwork Skills
Patrice Palmer

Classroom Community Builders—Activities for the First Day & Beyond
Walton Burns

50 Activities for the First Day of School
Walton Burns

The Open End—Stories for Learning, Discussion, and Expansion (forthcoming)
Taylor Sapp

Keeping the Essence in Sight (forthcoming)
From Practice and Observation to Reflection and Back Again
Sharon Hartle

We are a small, independent publishing company that specializes in resources for teachers in the area of English language learning. We believe that a good teacher is resourceful, with a well-stocked toolkit full of ways to elicit, explain, guide, review, encourage, and inspire. We help stock that teacher toolkit by providing teachers with practical, useful, and creative materials.

Sign up for our mailing list on our website, www.alphabetpublishingbooks.com, to find out about our new books, and for discounts and giveaways you won't find anywhere else.

HER OWN WORST ENEMY

A Serious Comedy About Choosing a Career

ALICE SAVAGE

Alphabet PUBLISHING

ISBN   978-1-948492-03-4 (paperback)
        978-1-948492-04-1 (epub)
        978-1-948492-05-8 (kindle)

Library of Congress Control Number: 2017964412

Country of Manufacture Specified on the Last Page

First Printing 2018

Published by:
Alphabet Publishing
1204 Main Street #172
Branford, Connecticut 06405 USA

info@alphabetpublishingbooks.com
www.alphabetpublishingbooks.com

Designed by James Arneson Art & Design, JaadBookDesign.com

All photographs licensed from Adobestock or Depositphotos, except as acknowledged below:

  Photograph of Steve Herbert page 24, courtesy of Steve Herbert
  Image of Mira Supercomputer page 24, by the Argonne National Laboratory / U.S. Department of Energy (public domain)
  Photograph of Molly Dill page 29, courtesy of Molly Dill
  Photograph of Wortham Theater, page 29, rkimpeljr (cc-by-sa-2.0 license)

Steve Herbert and Molly Dill were interviewed by the author in November, 2017. The author and publisher would like to thank them for their time.

*T*hank you to my family for loving theatre, especially Cyrus and Kaveh Shafiei because you remind me how much I love it, too.

I also want to thank the Carnegie Theater students for helping to workshop the script through readings and recordings. Cyrus, Jackson, Kaveh, Sadie and Viviana as well as Davis and Sam, you showed up and worked hard!

I am also extremely grateful to my colleagues at Lone Star College for believing in me, and for working with me on developing the material. Thanks, Amy, Anne, Colin, David, Erin, Janet, Joy, Katie, Macarena, and Masoud. You are all gifted teachers, and I love working with you!

Finally, I want to thank Ken Wilson for your wise counsel and Walton Burns for taking a chance on an unconventional manuscript. It has been a pleasure!

Contents

Introduction

THE LANGUAGE classroom is a great place for drama. When you produce a play, you combine both language and skills practice. You study vocabulary, grammar, and pronunciation. You also learn about conversations and develop strategies for interacting with others. Plays can demonstrate the phrases and expressions we use when we make friends, disagree with someone politely, offer praise, and reach other conversational goals.

In this book, you will have a chance to work on all these areas by preparing and performing a play. Through background readings and discussions, you will develop your vocabulary and explore the themes of the play. Through focused stress, intonation, and pronunciation work, you will learn to communicate the emotional intentions of your message, as well as learn the sounds of words in connected speech. Finally, through the production of a play, you will explore culture and language while performing the sometimes serious, sometimes funny, moments of the life of a young woman struggling with the decision of what to study in college.

A special feature of this book is the opportunity to work on something called **pragmatics**. Pragmatics describes the skill of getting messages across through the culturally appropriate use of language and gesture. Everyone uses pragmatics in their own language, but it is practiced in different ways among different communities. When people are good at the pragmatics of a language, they reach their goals without hurting their relationships. Here is an example:

Mike lives alone. He would like an invitation to a holiday dinner from his friend Lin. Mike says to Lin, "What are you doing for Thanksgiving?" Lin explains that she and her husband are having a few relatives over. "Oh, that sounds nice," says Mike. There is a pause. Lin says, "What are you doing for the holiday?" and Mike says, "Oh, nothing." There is another pause. Lin says, "Well, why don't come to our house? It's a simple gathering, but we'd love to have you." Mike is happy, "Oh, great!" he says, "Thank you so much. That's very kind of you!" and the conversation continues.

In this short exchange, Mike communicates his desire for an invitation indirectly. Mike cannot say, "Can I come to your house for Thanksgiving?" because that would not be polite. He would be putting Lin in an awkward position because it would be hard for her to say no. Instead, Mike creates the conditions for Lin to understand his situation. Then *she* can decide to invite him or not without feeling uncomfortable or rude.

In this instance, Mike is demonstrating good social skills, which is another way of saying he's good at pragmatics. However, this is only true if Lin is happy with the conversation as well. If Lin feels that Mike has pushed her to make the offer, she will use her own pragmatics skills to let him know that his efforts to get an invitation were inappropriate.

Pragmatics skills are most useful in challenging situations. These situations rarely appear in textbooks, which is why pragmatics is often considered a hidden language. In fact, people tend to need pragmatics most during uncomfortable or important conversations. In these cases, people with good pragmatics skills use special phrases to signal their intention. For example, look at the sentence, "I don't want you to take this the wrong way, but I don't think singing is for you."

The expression, *I don't want you to take this wrong way, but . . .* is a familiar signal in English. It is how you can warn someone that you are about to say something that is truthful, but not complimentary. When the listener knows criticism is coming, they can prepare for it. There are many of these signal phrases that you can use to feel in control of a conversation. A play is a good place to learn them because you can experience the expressions in a social and emotional context.

In addition to pragmatics, while working on the play, you will have opportunities to practice the more familiar skills of pronunciation. Because you will be speaking high frequency phrases used by family members and friends, you can work on natural tone, intonation, and gesture. You may notice that your voice goes up or down, or slower or faster, depending on the mood of your character. Sometimes you will try to speak in a joking way. At other times, you will show frustration or confusion.

Word and sentence stress will also be important. As you rehearse, you must make decisions about which content words to emphasize to best support your meaning. You'll say these words louder and clearer so the audience will understand. You'll also become aware of syllable stress in longer words. Having the right stress helps people recognize the word when you are saying it.

Finally, you'll have a chance to practice conversation skills when you read and discuss the topics in the background articles and prepare to perform the play. You'll share opinions, give reasons, make suggestions, offer and respond to advice, and provide encouragement to your peers. These are all useful academic and workplace abilities.

After the play, you will find additional activities you can do to use what you've learned in new ways. Hopefully, by the end of this book, you'll feel a little more confident about your English conversational skills, especially when talking about 21st century jobs and the struggles of young people to prepare for the future.

How to Use This Book

THE ACTIVITIES and ideas in this book are presented in a specific sequence. However, the book is designed to be flexible. For example, you may take a month or more to work on the play and the accompanying activities. A longer time frame can allow you to go deeper into research and skills development throughout the rehearsal period. Or you may take a week, skip over some of the activities, shorten rehearsal time, and have students read with a script in hand. Either way, students working in collaboration will benefit from their experience with conversational English.

The best way to plan your theatre production is to read through the script, activities, and background reading texts. Then decide on an approach that best fits your students' level, your curricular objectives, and your schedule. Also decide how much you will need to be involved in supporting the production. For some classes, the students may be able to do much of the work themselves.

You can mix and match the activities to fit your curricular objectives. There are texts that can be expanded to work on reading skills. There are writing prompts that allow students to analyze the topic from different perspectives. These can also be used as preparation for a mini-debate on the value of supporting the arts in society—a major theme of *Her Own Worst Enemy*. Some teachers might like to reserve part of the class for skills work and the other part of the class for rehearsal.

To plan the production, think carefully about your schedule. You want students to feel a sense of accomplishment at the end. Having students memorize lines, block, rehearse, and perform a play is rewarding but it takes an investment of time and energy. If you don't have the time, you can aim for a rehearsed reading and still reap many of the benefits. Also, for technology-adept students, you might want to support them in creating a video production which can be uploaded and watched by the class or otherwise shared.

There are a number of ways to adjust the materials to the level of your class. This module is designed for low intermediate to high intermediate levels. For lower levels, you might want to simply use the play as a text. You can do the activities and discuss the characters' decisions and the plot, as well as the topic of choosing a college major. Then you can have students practice reading the parts from the script to work on sounds and intonation. For middle levels, you might have students memorize and perform the play, but do a rehearsed or staged reading (see page 49 for some ideas on how to produce the play). To up the challenge for higher levels, do a full performance. Have students memorize lines and perform for another group, or even create a video to be shown to a wider audience. Also, feel free to allow students to adjust or even change lines to suit their goals.

There are other ways to be flexible with the script as well. If you have several groups stage the same play, consider having some of the groups rewrite a specific scene, such as the ending, or even write new scenes. This will allow them to be creative and keep the show fresh from one performance to the next. If groups produce different plays, you may want to start performances with a short introduction to the script's central issues. This can be done by the director as a way to help the audience follow the plot. In addition, you can change names in the script to reflect different genders or countries as needed. You can also add or double up roles. However, it is a good idea to have at least one person who does not act and can take on the role of director, videographer, and/or stage manager.

While students are rehearsing, you can circulate, take notes, and provide support as needed. You can also meet with each group to give specific feedback on pronunciation or scene work. Some groups may need more encouragement than others, but as long as the play is comprehensible and they have the language skills to communicate with each other, they should be able to produce a play with minimal support.

You also have choices on how you handle performances. Some teachers like to do all the plays on the same day, while others do one a day for two days. If your class is doing one play, you might perform for a different class, perhaps one at a lower level. In any case, allow at least 30 minutes for each performance, and consider doing a talkback or having classmates give feedback at the end. (See the post-performance section on page 57)

Finally, there are ideas for different types of assessment at the end of the book. If using a rubric such as the one on page 62, it is a good idea to give the rubric to the students at the beginning of the production so they know what you will value.

Most importantly, enjoy the process! Experiment. Think critically. Be creative. And above all, have fun!

SUGGESTIONS FOR DIFFERENT CLASS SIZES

Different classes have different numbers of students. This can present a challenge when producing a play, so here are some suggestions for making sure all students are engaged. By dividing the class into groups and giving each group a project, you can provide practice for everyone. One way to do this is to give students a preference sheet. Some may prefer to act. Others may prefer to participate in a debate.

Group option one: Produce the play

Group option two: Have a second group produce one of the other plays in Alphabet Publishing's Integrated Skills Through Drama series. Have the two groups perform for each other.

Group option three: Organize and have a debate based on the readings and possibly some outside research on the topic. See page 58. (See instructions and materials for structuring a mini-debate on the Alphabet Publishing website at http://www.alphabetpublishingbooks.com/integrated-skills-through-drama)

Group option four: Have one or two videographers make a documentary about the process. They can interview and film the actors as they prepare for their roles. Then the videographers can edit the video and share it with the class.

Group option five: Write and produce a short sequel to the play. Choose one of the following ideas or create your own. Create enough characters so that everyone has a role. See page 58 for ideas.

Preview

LOOK AT THE photo and discuss your answers to the questions below:

THINK ABOUT THE TOPIC

a. In your opinion, what are the best careers for college students today?

b. What career is most interesting for you? How did you decide?

c. Do you think a college major should be a family decision, or should the student make the decision on his or her own?

DISCUSS THE TITLE

What does *She is her own worst enemy* mean? Read the situations below. Which ones do you think fit the expression? Can you think of other examples?

- **a.** Po likes to play soccer, but he often gets angry and fights with other players. Now it is hard for him to find a team to play with.
- **b.** Lan wears very old clothes to job interviews because she does not think her appearance is important to employers.
- **c.** Jefta asks his older brother for help with his homework so he can do well on the test.
- **a.** Prima can never find her keys, so she is often late to appointments.

She is her own worst enemy

In English, we often use the phrase *She is her own worst enemy* or *He is his own worst enemy* when we think someone does something that is not good for them. Sometimes it is a habit or a personality characteristic that leads the person to make a poor decision. It is possible to say *You are your own worst enemy* to someone we know very well, such as a family member, but most often we use it to talk about someone who is not there.

We should also note that the people who say this may or may not be correct in their analysis.

WRITE ABOUT THE TOPIC

People usually like what they are good at, but what if they don't? What if someone has a talent for something such as sports or singing, but they don't want to develop it as a career? Should they do it anyway? Have you ever been in this situation? Do you know someone who has?

Discuss your ideas in groups. Then write a short paper with your answers to one or more of these questions. Try to use examples of someone you know to support your ideas. When you finish, share your thoughts with a partner.

The pragmatics of encouraging someone

Sometimes people see something valuable in another person, but that person cannot see it in themselves. In order to encourage the other person, a friend, partner, or family member might ask questions or make observations that help the person gain confidence.

Note that pragmatics in an informal family conversation is very different from pragmatics in a formal work or academic situation, so it is important to pay attention to the context so you can make informed decisions about what to say, how and when.

A wants to give B confidence.	*B is reluctant to accept an opportunity.*
MOVE 1: Bring up the topic. Greet B, exchange a few pleasantries. Then introduce your purpose. Say you heard about B's opportunity/challenge.	
	Acknowledge the opportunity. Then give reasons why you think it won't work.
MOVE 2: Ask questions to challenge B's thinking. Listen to B carefully and ask WH questions: • Why do you say that? • Where does this idea come from? • Why do you think you have this opportunity? • Truthfully, what is *really* making you nervous?	
	Listen to A and answer the questions honestly.
MOVE 3: Help B imagine a more positive view. Listen to B and try to guide B to a positive perspective with questions and observations. E.g., • What do you think it would be like to . . .? • If you did say yes, how would you . . .? • I remember how you handled . . . • I have noticed that . . .	
	Use A's guidance to explore new ways of thinking. Become more hopeful. Thank A for his/her help.

PRACTICE PRAGMATICS: ENCOURAGING SOMEONE

In this role play, B is unsure of their talent in a particular area. A is trying to encourage B by helping B talk through the issues.

1. Work with a partner. Choose a talent from the box below or think of your own idea. Then use the sentence stems that follow to create two or three sentences for each partner to say in the role play.

Talents			
Sports	Cooking	Drawing	Writing
Fixing things	Singing	Dancing	Playing music
Math	Sales	Childcare	Computers

Partner A: Encourage	Partner B: Express hesitation
You are really good at . . .	Thanks, everyone says that, but I'm not sure why. It's just luck. I think that . . .
Can you imagine yourself doing this for a career?	It's kind of a hobby for me, but I couldn't do it professionally because . . .
What do your friends/family members think?	People say . . ., but they're my friends, so of course they think . . .
What is holding you back?	The truth is that I don't think I'm that good. I'm just doing it because . . .
What might change your mind?	I don't know. Maybe if . . .

2. With a partner, choose roles, either **A** or **B**. Work with your partner to act out the situation for two minutes. Use the model in the instruction box above to guide your conversation.
3. Switch roles and repeat. You can also switch topics.
4. Discuss the experience. Does the language feel comfortable to you? Would you make different choices in your first language? Explain.

ADDITIONAL PRACTICE

1. Close your books and practice the conversation again. Listen to your partner and try to respond naturally.
2. Change partners and repeat.

READ FOR BACKGROUND

Choosing a college major is a challenge for the young woman in this play. In order to understand her decisions and actions, it is helpful to do some research on her choices.

Vocabulary

Match the phrases to their meanings. Look up words or expressions that you want to learn more about. Try to use them in new sentences or dialogs.

1. _____e_____ (figurative) to be in an unpleasant or ugly place; (literal) a ditch along a city street where rain and garbage collect.	a. face tough competition
2. _____ the creation of clothing for an actor or a musician	b. a potential solution
3. _____ the main focus of study in university	c. innovative activity
4. _____ to think about a topic that the public has opinions about or needs to make a decision about	d. (be) on the defensive
5. _____ when many talented or deserving people are trying to win a contest such as a race or get a reward such a job or a prize.	e. in the gutter
6. _____ to try very hard and not give up	f. costume design
7. _____ to protect one's views or position against someone who disagrees	g. to resemble an authentic situation
8. _____ acting like everyone else	h. have persistence
9. _____ a possible plan for fixing a problem	i. a college major
10. _____ an action or creation that is new and different	j. to try out different perspectives
11. _____ to be similar to something in real life	k. to explore a social issue
12. _____ to try to understand how other people think about a topic	l. conventional behavior

Read the article about STEM and the career profile. Highlight and take notes on important points. Then do the discussion tasks that follow.

A STEM Career

In the early days of the 20th century, a single smart and curious person could learn the mechanics of nearly every machine ever invented. They could understand the entire workings of the combustion engine, basic electrical systems, and radio waves. One hundred years later at the beginning of the 21st century, such a thought is impossible.

Technology experts often cite something called Moore's law to show how fast technology is changing our world. In the late 1970s a computer scientist named Gordon E. Moore made a prediction. He said that computing power would double every two years. Gordon's prediction has been true so far. As a result, machines are more powerful and more complex than anyone could have imagined even ten years ago.

All this progress has led to the growing importance of STEM fields. STEM stands for Science, Technology, Engineering, and Math. People who go into STEM fields study the physical and mechanical worlds. A person who goes into a STEM career has an opportunity to participate in solving problems and remaking the world around us. Examples of these changes include the voice recognition software that allows you to talk to a device such as your phone or computer, the satellite that sends you traffic updates, and exoskeletons that allow people with disabilities to walk.

Today, many universities have specialized programs in STEM fields. Here are some examples that are a little different from traditional engineering and science majors:

Biochemistry: Students learn about the chemicals that form life. They use this knowledge to create new medicines and cure diseases. For example, with a tool called CRISPR, biochemists can create specialized treatments for certain cancers and other genetic diseases.

Cybersecurity: Students learn to fight crime that happens on the Internet. When they are successful, they can stop a criminal from stealing people's information or shutting down power to a city.

Bioengineering: Students study nature's designs in order to make better machines such as walking robots inspired by the way insects move. They also work with the medical industry to create artificial body parts, some of which can be controlled by the brain.

Meteorology: Students study the weather. They use computer modeling to find out how the climate is changing and provide information that helps people make decisions. When storms come, they give warnings that can save lives.

Artificial intelligence: Students take various computer science, physics and other courses where they learn to create systems that are self-learning. Instead of writing software code for the computer operation, they create something called a neural net that learns in a way that is similar to the human brain.

People who are interested in a STEM career must be willing to study hard. Many people who declare a STEM major struggle to learn and apply new knowledge. However, those who persist can often find rewarding work in creating the inventions of tomorrow.

Discussion

Work in groups of three. Read and discuss the questions for five minutes. Then complete one or more of the sentences below to share with the class.

1. What technologies do people have today that we did not have 100 years ago? How about 10 years ago? What do you think will happen in the next 10 years?

2. Which STEM field is most interesting to you? Why?

STEM Career Profile: Steve Herbert

CEO, Nimbix, High Performance Cloud Computing

Steve Hebert always liked to build things. As a child, he used blocks, Legos, and other toys to make buildings. When he got older, Hebert became interested in making things with wood. He learned to use tools to help his father and brothers. One skill led to another, and he started taking things apart and putting them back together. He began with pens, moved on to watches, and then radios and other mechanical devices. His strong need to learn how things work changed his life, and he would end up in a career that did not exist when he was a child.

Steve Hebert

Hebert grew up at a time when technology was expanding faster than ever before in history. However, few people realized its potential. Most people thought computers were strange machines that were used only by researchers in labs and universities.

Hebert was not an ordinary person, however. With his desire to know how things work Hebert became interested in computer science. It was a fast-growing field, and it fit his passion for technology and all fields of discovery. He could see a connection between science and engineering and the possibility of creating solutions for solving difficult human problems.

Mira, a Blue Gene/Q supercomputer at Argonne National Laboratory, one of the fastest in the world.

When it was time for college, Hebert looked for the biggest challenge he could find. He found this challenge in electrical engineering. He says, "Electrical engineering was considered the hardest field of engineering at that time, and I wanted to take on the hardest field. Perhaps some of my own competitiveness was part of the reason. If someone else could understand how to build these amazing devices made from microscopic transistors, why not me?"

Hebert enrolled in Santa Clara University located in California's Silicon Valley which was just starting to attract attention. Computer engineers were building the first personal computers (PCs) in their garages. Santa Clara University and Stanford University as well as the University of California at Berkeley were investing in research. Hebert arrived to find a lot of innovative activity, and he wanted to be a part of it. At Santa Clara, he signed up for semiconductor device physics because it was the most difficult program within electrical engineering. Semiconductors are special materials that are essential to the working of all computers and electrical circuits. His decision to take on the challenge of understanding how computers work would allow him to play a role in the next wave of computer technology.

After working in the computer industry for many years, Hebert discovered supercomputing, linking computers together to form one giant, extremely fast computer. Supercomputers can take on bigger challenges in science and math than regular computers, and Hebert wanted to be a part of it. He and a partner decided to start their own company.

Now Hebert is the CEO (Chief Executive Officer) of Nimbix, a cloud-based service that offers powerful computing power. Cloud-based services use the Internet to make computers all over the world work together. Hebert says he did it for fun and because he loves the challenge. However, he also has a serious reason. He is realizing his dream of helping solve some of the most difficult human problems.

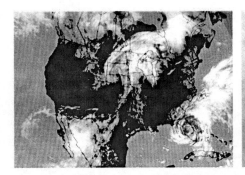  

Today customers use the Nimbix cloud computing service in different ways. Medical researchers use it to study human genes. They can use this information to find cures for disease. Energy companies research the weather or study oceans to find new sources of clean energy. Some customers even use the service to make art.

Many organizations also use supercomputing to "train" their computers. It is not yet possible for computers to think like a human, but powerful computers can connect new information with old information. They can also learn and improve. One example of this is facial recognition. Computers can identify individual faces and they get better as they add more data.

Hebert is an example of someone who found a passion for a STEM career early in life. He followed his interest and worked hard to achieve his goals. In reflecting on his inspiration, he talks about John F. Kennedy, the U.S. president who started the Apollo program that put humans on the moon. In a speech at Rice University in 1962, a few years before Hebert was born, Kennedy said:

We choose to go to the moon. We choose to go to the moon in this decade and do the other things, not because they are easy, but because they are hard, because that goal will serve to organize and measure the best of our energies and skills, because that challenge is one that we are willing to accept.

Hebert and many of his colleagues in STEM fields also want to take on hard challenges. As a result, they are changing the world. Since Hebert was born, computers have moved from the desk to our pockets, and even our watches. They will soon drive our cars and possibly do much of our work. While some people worry about the dangers of technology making certain people too powerful or replacing workers, Hebert does not worry. He is confident that new jobs will appear for his children's generation just as they did in his generation. "We need technology to solve the big problems like climate change and cancer. Computing will help us do that. There is no going back."

Discussion

Work in groups of three. Set a timer and talk for five minutes about one or more of the questions below. Then complete the critical thinking statements below.

1. Why is Steve Hebert's work rewarding?

2. What qualities or skills make him successful?

3. What kind of young person should go into this field?

4. What type of STEM career interests you? Why?

Insight sentences

1. This conversation made me think more about _____

_____

2. I realize that _____

_____

3. To be successful in STEM, a student should _____

_____

Next: Read the article about liberal arts fields and the career profile. Highlight and take notes on important points. Then answer the questions below. Discuss your answers with a partner.

A Liberal Arts Career

The term *liberal arts* sometimes confuses people because they think it is only about art, but the liberal arts include a diverse range of majors such as philosophy, political science, history, and economics, as well as visual and performing arts. These majors have something in common, however. They help people think about and understand humanity and our relationship to each other and the world.

A person with a liberal arts degree learns to tell a specific type of story. An economist studies how we exchange goods and services to create a financial story. A political science major looks at how we choose leaders to tell a government story. A historian tries to understand the past in order to tell stories about the present, and possibly to predict the future. And, yes, artists learn to tell stories that help us understand and share our individual and cultural experiences.

These stories help organize society. While different experts might add new elements or tell different stories, their work helps society understand itself, explore and develop new solutions to problems, and identify new ways to realize hopes and dreams.

A degree in the liberal arts can prepare a person for many different types of jobs. Some provide specific skill sets. Music majors learn to play an instrument, and drama majors learn to act, for example. However, a liberal arts degree can prepare students for any career including the law or business. This is because the liberal arts teach both specific knowledge and soft skills. Soft skills are abilities that people can use in many ways for many careers. For example, many liberal arts majors are valuable to employers across different industries because they have learned to do the following:

- communicate effectively in writing and speaking
- use empathy to understand people and their needs

 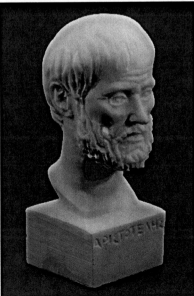 

- collaborate with others as teammates and managers
- look at problems from different perspectives in order to generate new solutions
- be flexible in their thinking and adapt to changing circumstances
- make connections between different types of information to create new ideas

While many liberal arts majors enter college with specific goals, others are not sure what job they will get in the future. However, research suggests that over the course of a career, a liberal arts major can do quite well in fields such as business and marketing or law as well as traditional areas such as teaching or fine arts. In fact, some experts suggest that the more creative majors are a good way to prepare for a future in which automation will do many jobs that humans do today.

Discussion

Work in groups of three. Read and discuss the questions for five minutes. Then complete one or more of the sentences below to share with the class.

1. What jobs are difficult for computers to do? Why?
2. What are some of the soft skills necessary for careers you are interested in?
3. What liberal arts field would fit with your personality and abilities?

Liberal Arts Career Profile: Molly Dill

Producing Director Houston Grand Opera

Molly Dill sits in on a dress rehearsal, the last chance to get the show right. This is the night before the opera version of William Shakespeare's *Macbeth* will open to the public. A preview audience sits in different parts of the enormous Wortham Theatre in Houston, Texas. Dill looks around. As a member of the opera company, she is nervous but hopeful. Then the curtain goes up and the show begins.

Molly Dill

The audience enters the story of Macbeth. At first, Macbeth is a young soldier, a hero in war. Other characters praise him, but in truth he has a flaw. When some witches predict that he will be a king, Macbeth begins to hunger for power. With some encouragement from his wife, Macbeth decides that his ambition is more important than his honor. The once good soldier takes a knife and murders his ruler, King Duncan. The audience sees him with the bloody knife and gasps in horror.

In the audience, Dill hears this gasp and breathes a sigh of relief. As producing director of Houston Grand Opera, she helped make this moment of horror, recognition, and empathy happen. She is one of hundreds of people who have given time, energy, creativity, and expertise to the goal of creating this moment. When it goes well, as it does tonight, the audience shares a particular experience of what it means to be human.

As audience members experience the opera, they explore various decisions, strengths, weaknesses, and motivations of the characters. In doing that, they also explore themselves and their own struggles with ambition and honor. Sitting in the darkness, they empathize with Macbeth, his wife, and the other characters, and they understand how a person might murder another and then be destroyed by guilt afterwards.

The Wortham Theater Center, home of the Houston Opera

Dill is fascinated by these moments of shared experience. It is why she loves her work organizing the various teams that create a production like *Macbeth*. These teams include dozens of singers, the eighty or so musicians, the team of directors, the stage hands, the set and costume designers, the lighting crew and many others who contribute to staging an opera. It is not easy work, but it is meaningful.

Dill got into theatre as a child when her best friend tried out for a school play. "I joined theatre so I could hang out with my friend," she says. In theatre, she discovered a sense of belonging. There were other kids like her that were interested in ideas and learning, and they were willing to work together to create something unique on the stage. Dill went on to attend Houston's High School for the Performing and Visual Arts, and then earn a degree in theatre arts from Webster University in Saint Louis.

Along the way, Dill decided she did not want to become an actress. She was beginning to realize the reality of an actor's life. First, she would need to learn specific technical skills. Second, she didn't want the pain of rejection after trying out for a part. Her arts training did, however, help her find what she was good at: administration. As an administrator, she works as a collaborator, a problem solver, and a vital part of the production. "No two days are ever the same," she says.

While Dill does not perform, she is grateful for the opportunity to participate in a shared experience of bringing an artistic vision to life. In fact, she likes doing it in the most challenging way possible. With opera, she has that challenge. "Sometimes I feel like I'm on the defensive," she says. "I mean opera, really? Does the world really need it?" Like many people in the arts, she understands that the role of art in society is a complicated one, but she tries to explain it. Opera combines visual arts, music, dance and theatre to create a vivid and emotional effect. When all the details are right, it connects people in a powerful shared experience.

Dill wants people to realize that while a well-received opera might seem like magic, it is not. "People do not always realize how technical art is," says Dill. "To be good, artists need to learn skills. They must study, practice, and improve." The entire process—from selecting the opera and researching the music and history to the development of the story and its message—requires learning. The process involves many conversations and decisions among the teams. How can they create a set or a costume that supports a common vision of an alien world? What do they need to learn to communicate the sadness of a lost love?

"I'm fascinated by the directors and how they work with the cast to help them to move from understanding to acting. Every detail matters," she says.

For Dill, this process means spending many hours in a dark theatre, but there are great rewards. She and others in the performing arts are able to think beyond their own knowledge and experience to generate something no one has ever done before. To explain, Dill likes to share a quote from the English writer Oscar Wilde, "We are all in the gutter, but some of us are looking at the stars."

If not for the arts and people like Molly Dill, we might not know those stars were there.

Discussion

Work in groups of three. Read and discuss the questions for five minutes. Then complete one or more of the sentences below to share with the class.

1. What soft skills are helpful in an opera production?

2. How is the work of producing an opera rewarding for Molly Dill and her colleagues?

3. Do you agree that society needs art? Explain.

4. What type of Liberal Arts career interests you? Why?

Insight sentences

1. This conversation made me think more about _____

   _____

2. I realize that _____

   _____

3. Employers need people with liberal arts backgrounds because _____

   _____

Attentive Listening

When people are collaborating on a project or a production, an important soft skill is listening to other's ideas. Good listeners understand and remember the ideas they hear. Then they respond to those ideas before they transition to their own ideas.

Use one of the stems below to rephrase the speaker's ideas.

- I like what you said about . . .
- So you want to make sure that . . .
- So, what you are saying is . . .
- My takeaway from this is . . .

To transition, use one of the stems below to add or comment.

- So, I want to add something to that.
- But don't you think . . .
- I really like what you say about . . . , and I also think . . .
- That makes sense as long as . . .

PRACTICE ATTENTIVE LISTENING: CHOOSE A CAREER

Choose a STEM or a liberal arts major. Then form groups of four or five for the speaking task below. Use the sentence stems provided or your own ideas.

a. Choose a timekeeper. The timekeeper sets a timer for four minutes and monitors the speakers to make sure they listen attentively.

b. One speaker begins by introducing his or her chosen major and explaining why it's a good major for the future.

c. Other group members respond, but each member must summarize what one previous speaker has said before continuing the conversation. The time keeper stops if anyone does not summarize the ideas of the previous speaker.

d. When the timer goes off, discuss your feelings about the activity. What was hard? What did you like? What was difficult? Also listen to the time keeper's comments.

e. Switch roles and repeat.

Her Own Worst Enemy

READ THE SCRIPT

Read the play. Make notes. Then discuss the questions that follow.

> THE PLAY takes place in and around the home of a family living in the United States. A high school senior, Aida Rivera, is preparing for college. Everyone has plans for her, but Aida has her own ideas. The play explores the question, "How do young people make good choices when it comes to choosing a college major?"

CAST

Marie Rivera: (mid 30s) Aida's mother

Laith Rivera: (late 30s) Aida's father

Lily Chen: (late 20s) Laith's sister

Ken Chen: (mid 30s) Lily's husband

Aida Rivera: (18) a senior in a U.S. high school (Note that Aida can be played by a male actor. Then his name would be Aiden.)

Vanessa Lewis: (17) Aida's friend (This role can also be played by a male. Then his name would be Van.)

Alan Horncastle: (late 30s) A theatre director at The Julliard School, a well-regarded college for the Performing Arts[1] (This role could also be played by a female. Then the name would be Alyssa)

Offstage Voice: This is a staff member at The Julliard School.)

Note: The characters are meant to be a combination of people from different cultural backgrounds. They were born in the U.S., but the cast can decide on the heritage countries.

---

1 The character of Alan Horncastle is not based on any real staff member of the Julliard School living or dead.

Other Roles

Director: This person manages the production, helps actors prepare in a way that supports the message of the play. The director may also introduce the play and lead the talkback after.

Stage manager: This person assists the director, organizes sets and set changes, manages special effects, such as the phone sounds, and turns off lights between scenes. The stage manager also reads the script silently along with the actors and gives lines if actors forget.

Videographer: This person videos the play and edits the video. They can work with groups individually to achieve close-ups and sound clarity. The Videographer may also interview cast members to create a documentary about the production as a side project.

Scene 1: *The Rivera family home. Evening. Marie Rivera, Laith Rivera, Lily Chen, and Ken Chen are all sitting around a dinner table stage right. They've just eaten a meal, and they are relaxing and chatting. Stage left, Aida and Vanessa are sitting on the floor and looking at their phones. They do not move or speak during this scene. Or they can be facing away from the audience.*

Marie: Aida doesn't know how talented she is.

Ken: She doesn't?

Marie: No, I don't think so. She can't see herself, can she? And she certainly won't believe me.

Lily: What do you mean, Marie? You're her mother.

Marie: It's complicated. I mean, Aida's just 17, right? And she's never seen herself on the stage, so she doesn't really know. How could she?

Ken: That's a shame. She really is good. I was amazed at the show tonight. Her performance was so deep. Seriously! I wasn't expecting much because it was just a high school production, but wow! It was like professional theatre!

Lily: Ken's right. She's brilliant. But she's good at a lot of things. She can do anything she sets her mind to.

Laith: (*Pleased*) Lily! That's nice of you to say so.

Lily: No, I mean it. You don't need to be modest, Laith. Aida is an amazing girl.

Marie: Yeah, I'm just sad that she doesn't want to do theatre anymore. She's quitting.

Ken: Noooooo! Please tell me you're kidding.

Marie: No, I'm not. It's true. She says she only did it because her friends were doing it.

Lily: Well, it's not so easy to be an actor in this world. Imagine all the auditions, all the rejections, all the waiting around for a director to call. I understand. Those things would be depressing!

Laith: (*Joking*) Yeah, maybe you're right. Aida says she wants to study biology or something like that, so we'll have to settle for a scientist in the family.

Marie: I suppose we can't complain. It's just hard to think that was Aida's last performance.

Ken: Maybe she'll change her mind.

Lily: And if she doesn't, she'll be a great scientist.

Marie: Yeah. (*She sighs.*) I just can't help being sad, you know?

(*The couples get up and leave the stage.*)

Scene 2: *The same house as scene 1, immediately after. The focus shifts to the living room where Aida and Vanessa are sitting. If they are facing away from the audience, they turn around. The girls put down their cell phones and start talking. They are close friends and feel comfortable teasing each other.*

Vanessa: They're talking about you, Aida.

Aida: I know.

Vanessa: Doesn't it bug you?

Aida: I'm used to it. I kind of tune them out.

Vanessa: Yeah. . . . parents.

Aida: They want me to do theatre in college.

Vanessa: You're kidding! That's great! My parents want me to get a real job. (*Vanessa uses two fingers of each hand to create air quotes around real job.*)

Aida: Your parents are smart.

Vanessa: Don't you want to do theatre?

Aida: No!

Vanessa: No?

Aida: No! They say it's my decision. But then they start talking about drama scholarships and stuff. It's making me crazy. There's no way I'm going to be an actor.

Vanessa: (*Surprised*) Seriously? You really don't want to?

Aida: Nah. It was fun. But I've got other plans. Anyway, how do they know if I have any talent? I'm their daughter. Of course they think I'm amazing.

Vanessa: Can I say something without you getting upset?

Aida: I don't know. What is it?

Vanessa: I think you're good, too.

(*Aida looks uncomfortable.*)

Aida: Now don't you start!

Vanessa: Yeah, yeah. . . . I get it. You've got other plans. But I can't help thinking. What if you get famous? Wouldn't it be great to be in the movies?

Aida: Vanessa! That's crazy talk. Look at me. Do I really look like a movie star?

Vanessa: Sure you do. . . . you could be a character actor. You're so funny!

Aida: Actually, I want a real job. (*Aida uses the same air quotes.*) I'm thinking about biology or maybe microbiology. My cousin Salma did a degree, and she's making a ton of money at a lab in Seattle or somewhere.

Vanessa: So that's medical-related, right? You're going to wear one of those white coats and look in a microscope all the time?

Aida: (*Rolls her eyes.*) Whatever! Yeah, well, maybe I will. That's what biochemists do. Or is it microbiologists. Anyway, something in medicine. I could be a nurse, too. You know what? I'd be love to be a nurse. They make a lot more money than actors. I'd be happy to be a nurse.

Vanessa: Most nurses make more money than most actors. That's true, but. . .

Aida: Can't you see me working in a hospital?

Vanessa: Yeah. . . . as an actress in a movie about a nurse who falls in love with her patient!

Aida: Really?

Vanessa: Really.

Aida: (*Defensively*) Well it's not going to happen! Look what happened to Lola! Do you remember Lola? She was a couple of years above us in school. She was a senior when we were just starting?

Vanessa: Oh yeah, she was so pretty and talented.

Aida: Yeah, well, that was when I was new in theatre, and I thought she was amazing. Everyone did. She went off to New York, and we all thought we'd see her in the movies. Well, you know what? I hear she's a waitress in a Greek restaurant.

Vanessa: She gets parts! I hear she was in a show last year.

Aida: Well yeah, but I bet she can't pay the rent. Anyway, it's not just the money. Nurses and scientists save lives! And what do actors do?

Vanessa: Make people cry?

Aida: Exactly!

Scene 3: The Rivera family home the next morning. Marie, Laith, and Aida are sitting together at the breakfast table.

Laith: Where's my phone?

Marie: I don't know. When did you last use it?

Laith: I don't know. I can't find it.

(*Aida pushes some buttons on her phone. A phone rings under some envelopes on the table.*)

Aida: Is that your phone?

(*Laith pushes aside the papers and sees his phone.*)

Laith: There it is! Did you just call me?

Aida: Yeah, What's this? (*Aida picks up an envelope.*)

Marie: It's your college mail. I was going to put it in your room.

Aida: Thanks, Mom. (*She picks up an envelope and opens it.*) Have you ever heard of Julliard?

Marie: (*Calmly, but excited*) Uh huh, it's in New York.

Aida: This says something about an audition. What kind of school is Julliard?

Laith: I'll look it up. Julliard, two *l*'s. Um. . . hang on a second.

(*Laith looks up the school on his phone.*)

Laith: It's a performing arts school in New York. Oh yeah, Julliard. I've heard of it. Lots of famous actors and musicians go there. (*Looks at his phone.*) Viola Davis went there. Wasn't she in that movie about that singer. What was her name?

(*Aida tosses the envelope back on the table and rolls her eyes.*)

Aida: I gotta go mom. I have a test tomorrow.

(*Aida gets up and leaves the table. Marie picks up the envelope and opens it. She reads the letter. She looks more and more surprised as she reads.*)

Laith: What is it? Are you okay?

Marie: This isn't junk mail, Laith. This is a personal letter from a teacher. At least I think it is. Look!

(*Marie hands the letter to Laith. Laith looks at the page. Laith and Marie freeze. The theatre director, Professor Alan Horncastle appears. He approaches the front center of the stage to speak the words in the letter.*)

Horncastle: Dear Ms. Aida Rivera, On the recommendation of your theatre teacher, a good friend of mine, I was able to see your performance in the play *Steel Magnolias* last weekend at your school, and I was impressed. You have very good instincts as an actress. Of course, it takes more than natural ability to be a truly great stage or film actor, which is why I'd like to personally invite you to audition at Julliard. We have trained a long list of successful theatre artists, and we are always on the lookout for the next generation of talent. We select a small number of applicants each year, and I think you might have the qualities we are looking for. If you are interested, please contact admissions below.

(*Horncastle leaves the stage. Laith and Marie look at each other silently.*)

Scene 4: *The Rivera family car. A few days later, in the afternoon. Aida and Vanessa are in the backseat, and Laith pretends to open the front door and get in the driver's seat. (This can be created through the placement of chairs.) Laith has his keys in his hand. He starts to put them in the ignition.*

Laith: Wait a sec. I forgot something.

Aida: Your phone?

Laith: Uh yeah. . . . I thought I had it.

(*Laith motions opening the door and getting out of the car.*)

Aida: (to Vanessa) You know we're trapped.

Vanessa: What do you mean "trapped"? Like we can't get out? I just need a ride home.

Aida: Well, my dad likes to talk in the car. He knows I can't leave.

Vanessa: What's wrong with that? My dad talks in the car.

Aida: Normally it's fine, but now he only talks about this theatre school called Julliard. Have you ever heard of it?

Vanessa: Uh, yeah! It's like only the most famous acting school in the country!

Aida: Really? Well, that really scares me.

Vanessa: Why? You don't want to go. . . . (*Vanessa hesitates when she sees Aida's face.*) Do you?

Aida: Well, they invited me to audition. I guess it's a big deal to be invited.

Vanessa: So go!

Aida: I'd just be wasting my time. . . . And theirs. . . . Shh. He's coming.

Vanessa: And you don't want to go?

Aida: No, I don't. I don't want to think about it. I don't want to talk about it. And I don't want to hear about it. . . . Now quiet. Here he comes.

(*Laith gets back in the car.*)

Laith: All set?

(*Laith turns on the engine and motions as though he is driving.*)

Laith: So, Vanessa. Did Aida tell you about her letter?

Vanessa: Yes, Mr. Rivera.

(*Vanessa makes eye contact with Aida. Aida sinks down in her seat.*)

Laith: So, what do you think? Shouldn't she go?

Vanessa: Well, yeah, I mean, if she wants to.

Laith: It's an amazing opportunity!

Aida: But dad, I don't want to be an actress!

Laith: Why don't you want to be an actress?

Aida: Because I'm going to study biology, microbiology, like Salma.

Laith: Like Salma? Your cousin?

Aida: Yeah, isn't she a scientist.

Laith: I think she's a teacher now, I mean at a university. (*Laith looks out the window and then brakes. They all jerk forward and back.*) Oops! I passed your house, Vanessa.

Vanessa: That's okay. I can walk.

Laith: Sorry, I got distracted. It's Aida's fault. She's making me crazy.

Aida: Dad, you're the one making *me* crazy!

(*There's a pause while Vanessa pretends to open the car door and get out.*)

Vanessa: Thanks, Mr. Rivera. Bye, Aida.

Aida: Bye, Vanessa.

(*Laith pretends to drive again by miming hands on the wheel.*)

Laith: Aida. . .

Aida: Dad, stop. I don't want to talk about it.

Laith: It's just an audition.

Aida: Please, Dad!

Laith: Think about it. It's only a weekend in New York. Just you and your mom. You can see some shows, go shopping. You'd like that, right? And then just one afternoon, you go to Julliard. No big deal.

Aida: (*Frustrated*) Dad. I'm about to open the door and jump out of the car.

Laith: Okay, okay, okay. . . I'll stop. I just want to say one last thing.

Aida: Last thing!

Laith: If you go, and you don't like it, I promise never to mention it again.

Aida: Promise?

Laith: Promise. I won't mention the word theatre or acting ever again.

Aida: Are you sure?

Laith: Yes. . . trust me. At least not in the same sentence as your name.

Aida: (*Resigned but perhaps secretly okay with it.*) Okay, I'll do it. But only if you promise never to talk about it again. Ever, ever, ever.

Laith: Never, ever, ever. Only cells, molecules, microscopes, and labs. I promise!

Aida: Alright, I'll go.

Scene 5: New York City. A few weeks later. A meeting room at Julliard in the afternoon. Aida and Alan Horncastle are standing next to a conference table. Marie is sitting in the corner, watching and wanting to talk but keeping quiet. She may start to say something even, but she always manages to stop herself.)

Horncastle: We can wait in here. They'll call you for your audition in a few minutes.

(*Aida nods. She is nervous. She taps her foot, plays with her hair or otherwise shows her anxiety about the upcoming audition. There is silence for a moment.*)

Horncastle: We do table work in here.

Aida: What's table work?

Horncastle: (*Surprised*) Ah, table work is where the play finds itself.

Aida: The play finds itself? What does that mean, "The play finds itself"?

Horncastle: A play is just words on a page. In table work, you sit with the director and figure out what those words mean. You study the history around the play and you think about the writer's message. Then as actors, you decide how you feel when you say the words.

Aida: Oh. I see.

Horncastle: You know, sometimes people say one thing and mean another. The same is true on the stage. As an actress, you might say something because you are angry or scared, but it's not what you really want to say.

Aida: (*Pauses*) I never thought about it like that.

Horncastle: Really? You were so good as M'lynn in Steel Magnolias. I was visiting your director and I saw the last performance, you know. When your daughter died, you made it seem so real! I was sure you had prepared.

Aida: Oh, that was just luck.

Horncastle: Do you really think so?

Aida: (*lying*) Yeah, I didn't really think about it that much.

Horncastle: Maybe you didn't need to think. You just had to become M'lynn.

Aida: Mr. Horncastle, I really appreciate your time here, but I promised my father I'd come just to make him stop pressuring me. I really can't be an actress. I don't know the first thing about acting. (*She hesitates.*) Besides, I need a real job.

Horncastle: A real job?

Aida: Right. It's fun to do plays, but everyone knows actors don't make any money. I'm not dumb enough to think I can be Hollywood's next big star.

Horncastle: So you feel like you'd be wasting your time if you chose to study theatre?

Aida: Well, don't take this the wrong way, but I'm a practical person. The thing I like about science is that I can count on it. It's real. You have a problem and you fix it. No one's watching you.

Horncastle: I'm trying to understand here. You see yourself as a scientist.

Aida: Well, not exactly, but medical professionals are more, you know, solid. (*She hesitates.*)

Horncastle: Necessary?

Aida: I'd be needed.

Horncastle: I don't know. (*He shrugs.*) I don't know what we'll need in the future. Machines and computers are doing a lot of work these days.

Aida: That's what my aunt Lily says. She says robots are going to do all our jobs.

Horncastle: Not all jobs. For example, can you imagine a robot actor?

Aida: (*Laughs*) Well, with special effects, why not?

Horncastle: (*Dramatically, as if giving a speech in a play.*) We can use technology, sure, but we've always needed actors and we always will. People come to the theatre to feel. They want to connect with the characters on an emotional level. They want to find out what happens when people make certain kinds of decisions. And these are decisions robots would never make. That's where comedy comes from!

Aida: (*Interested. She understands what he is saying.*) And tragedy! The sad stuff.

Horncastle: Exactly! Science explains life. It even makes life possible, but theater . . . Theatre makes life matter.

Aida: Okay, okay. I see what you're saying but I don't see myself in that way. When I get on stage, I just do it. I don't feel like I have talent at all. I feel like I'm fooling people, like I'm a fake and no one has figured it out yet.

Horncastle: Aida . . . I can completely understand. It's natural to feel like a fake sometimes. You don't have much experience. You're thinking that acting is some sort of magical gift, like you have it or you don't.

Aida: Well, isn't that true?

Horncastle: Sure, some people are born with natural talent, but a lot of it is just committing to your art. We can help you turn natural talent into a reliable skill set.

Aida: That's hard to believe.

Horncastle: I've been doing this a long time, Aida. It's not magic; it's a job, just like being a doctor is a job. At least that is how we approach it here at Julliard. We expect you to go out and be employed as a working actor.

Aida: That just seems impossible to me.

Horncastle: Of course. (*Looks at his watch.*) Look, we're getting close. Let me leave you here so you can prepare for your audition. Do your breathing exercises. You don't have to decide now, but when you do, we want you to be one hundred percent sure.

Aida: Thank you Mr. Horncastle.

(*Horncastle leaves. Aida sits facing the audience. She closes her eyes and takes slow deep breaths.*)

Offstage Voice: Aida Rivera

(*Aida opens her eyes.*)

Scene 5: *New York City. A hotel room later that night. Aida is sleeping stage left. Marie comes and to look at her.*

Marie: (*Whispers*) Aida? Are you asleep?

(*Aida rolls over and sighs. She does not wake up. Marie leaves. Laith, Lily, Vanessa and Horncastle all walk out and stand in a row facing the audience. Each speaks in turn.*)

Vanessa: I think it's so cool that you can be an actress, but I don't understand you. If I were you, I'd jump at the chance. I don't even know why it's a question.

Lily: You are smart to follow your instinct. Science is a much more practical career. You can get a job, earn money, support your family. . . live a normal life.

Laith: I am so proud of you! You can really be someone, Aida. Just think! You can make so many people happy with your art!

Ken: It seems to me like you are your own worst enemy! You should just do what you love. I think you love theatre, but I'm just your aunt's husband. What do I know?

Horncastle: Acting is hard work. You've got to commit yourself to the process. It's not some magical gift. There are real things that you can learn to transform yourself on the stage, but you have to choose it.

(*The characters leave the stage. Aida sits up, shakes her head, and puts her head in her hands.*)

Scene 6: *An airport back in Aida's city two days later. Laith is at the airport. He paces up and down. He takes out his phone and looks at it. Then he puts it back. He walks some more. He is clearly agitated. Finally, he gets a call.*

Laith: Hello? Has your plane landed?

(*Pause*)

Are you here?

(*Pause*)

How was the trip?

(*Pause*)

What?

(*Pause*)

Can you hear me now?

(*Pause*)

Okay, okay, I'm at baggage claim.

(*Laith hangs up. He continues to pace. Marie and Aida appear.*)

Laith: Hi (*He greets his wife and daughter.*)

Marie: Hi, sorry we were late.

Laith: Uh huh. No worries. (*He looks at Aida.*) How was New York?

Aida: It was good, kind of cool in the mornings. Lots of steam coming up off the sidewalks and I didn't know it would smell. New York has a million smells!

Laith: You know, I never thought about that. I guess you can't know New York until you smell it. But did you like it? What did you think? What did you think of Julliard?

Aida: It's okay, I guess. They were really nice and all. But I don't think it's for me.

(*Laith looks at Marie. Marie shrugs.*)

Laith: So you really want to go into microchemis—something . . . what is it?

Aida: Microbiology. Yes. And now that I've gone to Julliard and I've done everything you asked, you promised never to talk about it again.

Laith: (*Lifts hands in a gesture of tired resignation.*) Okay Aida. You win. Your mother and I will support you whatever you choose.

Aida: It's not that bad, dad.

Laith: (*Joking*) I'm going to call you when I'm an old man and my back hurts.

Marie: (*Also joking*) That's not what microchemists do.

Aida: Microbiologists.

Marie: Microbiologists. They all seem kind of similar. Small stuff, right?

(*Aida rolls her eyes.*)

Aida: Hang on a second. I have a text. (*Aida looks at her phone. Then her face changes. She's excited.*)

Aida: I just got a text from Mr. Horncastle.

Marie: What?

Aida: He wants me to call him.

Marie and Laith: (*At the same time*) Why? What is it?

(*Aida walks away. She talks on the phone.*)

Laith: Do you think we should try and get a tutor or something? She hasn't taken a lot of science classes.

Marie: Let's talk to Lily. She'll have some ideas. If Aida doubles up on science courses in her first two years, maybe she can catch up.

Laith: I have to admit I'm disappointed, but we should be grateful. She is going to be a great macrobiolochemistist.

Marie: Microbiologist, Laith. I guess we need to stop teasing her. If she wants to be a microbiologist, we need to help her make that happen.

Laith: Agreed. (*Slowly*) Mic–ro–bi–ol–o–gist. It has a nice sound. She'll probably be rich. Don't they make medicine?

(*Aida walks back with a thoughtful look.*)

Aida: Um. I think I might have just made a huge mistake.

Laith: What kind of mistake?

Aida: Well, Mr. Horncastle just offered me a spot at Julliard.

Laith: (*He sighs.*) And you turned him down, right?

Aida: Actually, Dad, I didn't. I decided if they wanted me, there must be a reason.

Marie: What are you saying?

Aida: I'm saying. . . Well, I guess I'm saying. . .that I said I'd think about it. I mean I think we need to sit down and discuss it. What do you think? I know I was set on science, but then when it came down to it. I couldn't say no to theatre. In fact, I never seem to be able to say no to theatre.

Laith: And you can say no to science?

Aida: Well I guess I already have or I would have studied it more. I guess I like the *idea* of being a scientist, but not the actual *work*.

Marie: Well science is not exactly how you spend your time.

Aida: No, it's not. Something in me keeps going back to theatre. I thought I hated it, but Uncle Ken is right, I love it. I'm just afraid. What if I fail?

Marie: But Julliard wants you.

Aida: So maybe I am good at it…

Laith: That's my girl! You've got the theatre bug. So now we're done. We've had the discussion. You can call him back.

Aida: What? Now?

Laith: Sure, no time like the present. You might as well call that Horncastle guy before he offers the spot to someone else. Take a chance! Tell him yes!

(*Aida looks at her mother. Marie nods and smiles. Aida takes out her phone and begins to make a call.*)

[Curtain]

DISCUSS THE PLAY

Talk about the play in groups. Share your analysis with the class.

1. Why does Aida change her mind?

2. Why do you think Aida's parents want her to do college theatre?

3. How is Lily's advice different from Ken's advice? Which one do you agree with?

4. How do you describe Aida's relationship with her parents? Is it similar to or different from family relationships in your life?

5. Does Aida make a good choice in your opinion? Why or why not? Would you make a similar choice if you were her?

Production

▶ **PERFORM THE PLAY** for your class or another class. You may also choose to film your play. You may also want to have the audience read along or not. Here are some suggestions for rehearsing and performing.

a. **Rehearsed reading:** Actors work with a director and the script. Then they read the parts with a focus on emotion, stress, and intonation.

b. **Staged reading:** Actors work with a director and the script. They also block the play. However, in the performance, they carry and read from a script.

c. **Full performance:** Actors prepare their roles, memorize their lines and block the play. They perform for an audience just like in a real theatre. There can be an intermission in which audience members can reflect or ask questions, or the play can continue to the end.

d. **Video:** Work with a videographer to record the performance and then edit the video. Then watch it later with your teacher, your group or the whole class.

ANALYZE THE PLAY

Read the play again. Answer the questions by taking a few notes on your own.

The Story	Notes
The main character of a story always has a conflict. Who is the main character in this story, and what is the conflict?	
A play often deals with a serious social issue. What is the social issue in this play? What groups in society are affected by it?	

The Story	Notes
Even a serious play can have comic moments. Comedy often comes from an unexpected action. People might not behave in a conventional way. In what way is this play funny?	
A play should be believable. The audience should empathize with one or more characters. Do you feel similar to any of the people in the play? Explain.	

ASSIGN ROLES

Decide who will play which character. There are two ways to do this.

- Give the director/teacher the names of two or three characters you are willing to play. Then that person will assign you a role.

- Audition for a part. Give the director/teacher the names of two or three characters you are willing to play. Then read part of the play as that character with another student to show your skills. The director/teacher will then assign roles based on who does the best job of acting the different characters.

LEARN YOUR PART

Read the play again and highlight your lines in yellow. Then make decisions about your character's personality and emotions. The tasks below will help.

1. Read the vocabulary describing emotional states and the first example. Write a second example from your own experience or research.

	Example one	Example two
admiring	Lulu thinks Star is a talented musician and sees all her performances.	*My uncle is a doctor. Everyone in the family respects him because he helps people and he is successful.*
careless	Remi always forgets to return Ty's phone calls.	

cautious	Tish checks all the doors before she leaves the house.	
confident	Ping volunteers to be the speaker because he thinks he is a good presenter.	
defensive	Jo refuses to take responsibility for the car accident, but the police gave her a ticket.	
empathetic	Lois is sad because her friend lost his job.	
frustrated	Myra's father can't understand why Myra doesn't study even when he asks her to.	
humor	Lan walks into a tree while he is texting. He does not get hurt, but his friends laugh.	
insecure	Bao is afraid to speak to a girl he likes because she might not like him.	
patience	Ari's mother waits several months for Ari to look for a job.	
resigned	Sue stops trying to change her parents' mind about her tattoo.	
secretive	Dana whispers the news in Sheila's ear so her classmates can't hear.	
teasing	Rob tells his wife he forgot her birthday. Then he gives her a gift. She laughs.	

2. Decide how your character feels in your scenes and use the vocabulary from the chart above or your own ideas to make notes on your script.

3. Memorize your lines. Choose from the following strategies. It will take several rehearsals to remember everything. Overlearn your part so you do not forget later.

- Read your part out loud two or three times a day.

- Record yourself saying the lines. Listen to the recording and try to improve your pronunciation, speed, and volume. You'll need to speak loudly and clearly in performance.

- Read while standing. Think about your movements and your tone of voice.

- Read with a friend who can say the other characters' lines.

REHEARSE

Read the play with other actors, and talk about your character's relationships with other characters.

1. Use the sentence stems below or your own ideas to discuss your motivations.

In this scene,

I want to hide my true feelings.	I'm getting very frustrated with you.
I don't want to upset you.	I want to change the subject.
I respect you.	You are making me uncomfortable.
I want to encourage you.	I am realizing something I hadn't thought of before.
I'm afraid.	I'm excited or nervous.
I'm telling you a secret.	I'm pretending I don't care.

2. Reflect on your pragmatics by discussing the following questions at the end of the rehearsal.

- How do other characters respond to you? Does it feel natural?

- How do your pragmatics choices make the play funny or serious? Do you want to try saying something in a different way?

- Would you make the same language choices if you were in this situation in your life?

Improv

Improv is short for improvisation or the art of making something up or finding solution in the moment. In theatre, improv activities help actors prepare for roles by acting out scenes without a script. The actors pretend to be their characters but they make up their lines.

Through improv they can:
- get to know their character's personality better
- understand their character's relationship to other characters
- be *in the moment* so the scene feels like real people talking to each other
- discover the physical mannerisms of their character (For example, an important woman might flick her eyes at someone's feet before looking at their eyes as a way to show power.)
- overcome stage fright and get comfortable in front of an audience

3. Improvise a conversation between two characters from the play. Here are some suggestions, or you can invent your own.
   - Alan Horncastle talks to Marie and Laith Rivera after the audition.
   - Marie and Aida have dinner in New York after the audition.
   - Aida calls her friend Vanessa to tell her about her decision to go to Julliard.
   - Marie tells Lily and Ken about Aida's decision.
   - Ken gives Aida advice before her audition.
   - Lily talks to Aida about her decision.

PRACTICE PRONUNCIATION: WORD AND SENTENCE STRESS

Work on finding the right stress and intonation. Also identify and practice any specific sounds that you have trouble with.

Sentence Stress

In sentences, important words such as nouns, verbs, and adjectives are stressed. We say them louder and longer. Small "function" words such as articles and prepositions are not stressed, so they are more difficult to hear. Here are some examples from the play. The **boldfaced** words are stressed. Think about the feelings in each sentence and how stress communicates those feelings.

I was **amazed** at the **show tonight**. Her **performance** was **so deep!**
We'll have to **settle** for a **scientist** in the **family**.

- There's **nothing wrong** with **working** in a **hospital**
- What do you mean "**trapped**"?
- I'm about to **open** the **door** and **jump** out into **traffic**.
- **Machines** and **computers** are doing **a lot of work** these **days**.

Notice that emphasizers (*so, a lot of*) may be small but they can be stressed to make an impression on the listener.

   a.   Practice saying the examples in the box above out loud. Then make corrections.

Word Stress

When words have two or more syllables, hearing stress on the wrong syllable can make the word incomprehensible for listeners, so it is also important to learn the stress of longer words. In the following examples, the stressed syllable is underlined, but some dictionaries capitalize or bold-face the stressed syllable, or they put a dot over it.

It's **just** an au<u>di</u>tion
Do your <u>brea</u>thing <u>exer</u>cises.
You don't have to de<u>cide</u> now.
We want you to be one <u>hun</u>dred per<u>cent</u> sure.
I **really** ap<u>pre</u>ciate your **time** here, but I **promised** my <u>fa</u>ther I'd **come** just to **make** him stop **pressuring** me.
Okay, okay, I'm at <u>bag</u>gage **claim**.

   b.   Go over your lines and mark nouns, verbs, adjectives and adverbs that you want to stress. Use a dictionary to identify and mark the stress of longer words.

   c.   Use a recording device such as your phone to record yourself saying the lines out loud. Listen and make adjustments.

   d.   Practice saying your lines with the other actors in the play. Help each other with intonation, pronunciation and stress. Speak loudly and clearly.

STAGE YOUR PLAY

Decide on how you will move during the play, where you move and when. Also think about how your character might show feelings through things like posture.

Blocking a play

When a director and actors prepare for a performance, they plan where people will stand, sit, and move. This is called blocking. Here are some basic guidelines that can help you create a successful performance.

- All actors should avoid speaking with their backs to the audience.
- All actors should speak loudly and clearly, not rush through lines.
- When one actor is speaking, all other actors should look at the speaker. They should not move or attract attention in any way.
- Actors should behave as if the story is happening to them for the first time and they are in a real conversation. Good acting is not reciting memorized lines. It's about reacting to other actors with interest and emotion.
- Actors should not make eye contact with the audience.

Notes on stage directions:

- Stage right means the right side of an actor who is looking at the audience. Stage left means the left side of the actor who is looking at the audience. Front and back also describe directions from the actor's position.
- To show a scene change, it is helpful to have someone turn off the lights for a short time. Actors use this dark time to change locations.

1. Block the play with your director. Here are some ways actors communicate emotions. Try acting them out. What does each of the following gestures communicate?

   - Fold your arms across your chest
   - Put your hands on your hips
   - Hold up your hands, palms outward
   - Sit and look up at a speaker/ Stand and look down at a speaker
   - Play with a phone or look away
   - Stand with a straight back
   - Stand with a bent back
   - Walk up and down the stage

- Put your hands over your eyes or in your hair
- Cover your mouth
- Put your hand over your heart.
- Bow your head
- Tilt your head to the side
- Shake your head
- Roll your eyes
- Sigh loudly
- Bite your lip
- Make your hands into claws
- Look at someone's feet then their face.

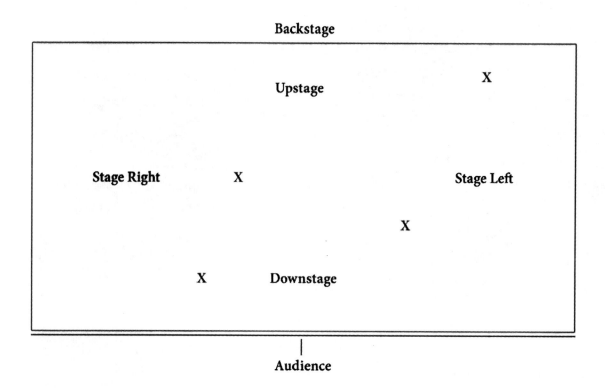

2. After blocking, practice several times. When you practice a lot, you will make fewer mistakes, and you will be less likely to break character during your performance. (Breaking character happens when you laugh or do something that takes you out of your role.)

Note: When you are rehearsing or performing, a stage manager can sit next to the stage and read the script silently while you perform. Then they can read you a line if you forget.

Post-Performance

THE FOLLOWING activities can be used to explore the themes and language with the audience after a production.

LEAD A TALKBACK

The director/teacher leads the class in a conversation about the play between the actors and the audience. There are many ways to do this but the following process is helpful.

a. There is a five-minute break after the play ends while audience members take a few minutes to write some questions. Here are some examples:

- How did you prepare for your role?
- Do you think Aida's parents are typical?
- Why do you think your character . . .?
- Do you think the father made mistakes about the type of science on purpose?
- How does the ending fit with the title?
- Why do you think Aida fought against becoming an actress?

b. The director and actors come out on stage and face the audience. The director invites questions and comments. The audience asks about the play or the characters, and the actors answer. People can direct their questions to individual actors.

WRITE AN ALTERNATIVE ENDING

Break up into groups and discuss other possible endings. Answer the questions. Then write your own dialogue.

a. What happens in the new ending?

b. Why does it happen?

c. How will it affect the lives of the different people involved?

d. Which is a better ending for the characters?

Perform your new ending for another group. Which ending is more believable and why?

GATHER LANGUAGE

Go through the script one more time and circle phrases and stems that you want to remember for when you have important conversations:

- Encouraging/responding to encouragement
- Giving advice/receiving advice
- Teasing a friend/responding to teasing
- Talking through an issue/supporting someone talking through an issue
- Praising/receiving praise

Note: Remember to pay attention to language used in casual situations between friends and in more formal situations between a professor and a student.

HAVE A MINI DEBATE

Form two teams and a panel of judges. One team thinks Aida made the right decision. The other team thinks Aida made the wrong decision. Each team gets a turn to make an argument. Then the other team gets a chance to respond and make a counterargument. You may have three or four rounds of argument and counterargument. The judges can individually write down up to five points for each team at the end of each round. When the debate is over, the judges meet to add their points and declare a winner.

See instructions and materials for structuring a mini-debate on the Alphabet Publishing website at http://www.alphabetpublishingbooks.com/integrated-skills-through-drama/.

CREATE A SEQUEL

Work with a partner or in small groups. What do you think Aida's life will be like in the future? Pick a time, such as five or ten years from now and write a short play about Aida's life. You may want to invent new characters. Here are some ideas, or you can invent your own.

- Five years later, Aida comes back to her high school class reunion. She talks to different people about their career choices, and they describe what they are doing and how they feel. (Students can research different careers for each character.)
- Ten years later: Write about a day in Aida's life as an actress. First, she has an interview with a reporter. Then she meets her parents for dinner, and they talk about their lives now.
- Ten years later: Vanessa has gone into a STEM field. Aida visits her, meets Vanessa's family, and Vanessa shares about her work. Perhaps her husband is also in a STEM field.

- Twenty years later: Aida's daughter is getting ready for college. She is trying to choose the right major, but she is not sure. Aida and her husband try to encourage their daughter. They share their stories and give advice. Their daughter may or may not agree with it.

Assessment

CHOOSE FROM the following assessments to reflect and give/get feedback on the experience. You can photocopy the forms in this book or go to http://www.alphabetpublishingbooks.com/integrated-skills-through-drama for downloadable versions.

TEACHER EVALUATION RUBRIC

Evaluation Rubric for *Her Own Worst Enemy*

Actor's name: _____

Check all boxes that apply. Assign one score for each row in the left column.
Add the two scores for a final score.

	High 50 – 46	**Middle 45 - 38**	**Low 37 - 0**
Preparation and Performance /50	☐ has memorized all lines ☐ speaks clearly with appropriate volume ☐ is believable in the role (pragmatics) ☐ responds to other actors naturally	☐ occasionally relies on script or prompting ☐ speaks so audience can comprehend most lines ☐ is mostly believable in the role (pragmatics) ☐ responds to other actors naturally most of the time	☐ uses script ☐ speaks quietly or quickly so it is difficult to understand. ☐ is not believable or breaks character, e.g., by laughing ☐ unnatural response to other actors
	Hight 50 - 46	**Middle 45 - 38**	**Low 37 - 0**
Language delivery /50	☐ conveys emotions through intonation and gesture ☐ uses effective sentence and word stress ☐ has consistently comprehensible pronunciation	☐ uses intonation and gesture ☐ uses sentence and word stress ☐ has mostly comprehensible pronunciation	☐ lack of intonation and gesture weaken emotional message ☐ has trouble with sentence and word stress ☐ has pronunciation issues that make comprehension difficult.

Total
  /100

PEER FEEDBACK GUIDE

1. Ask another actor questions to learn more about their performance.

    a. What were your goals in creating your character and preparing for the performance?

    b. What did you enjoy about the process?

    c. What was hardest for you?

    d. Did you develop any skills? Explain.

2. Tell the actor about your experience watching the play. You may use the stems below or your own ideas.

    a. My impression was that your character felt . . .

    b. My favorite part was when . . .

    c. I'd like to know more about . . .

    d. The play made me think about . . .

SELF-REFLECTION

Actor's name: _____

Write three or four sentences explaining your answers to the questions below.

1. How did you prepare for your role?

2. Did anything happen that surprised you?

3. Did your language and/or conversation skills improve? Explain.

4. How do you feel about your performance?

5. What advice would you give to other actors?

Beyond the Classroom

RESEARCH AND WRITE A CAREER PROFILE

 INTERVIEW SOMEONE and write a career profile

1. Do research

Choose one of the following activities:

☐ Interview a person with an interesting job and take notes. Consider the following questions and/or write your own.

- How did you get interested in this field?
- Who influenced you?
- How did you prepare for this career?
- How did you get your first opportunity in this field?
- What do you like best about your work?
- What skills do you have?
- What advice do you have for someone who wants to do this kind of work?
- Can you share a quote or person that shaped your thinking?

☐ Use the internet to find one or more videos of a famous person being interviewed in English about his or her work. Be sure to put the link to the video(s) on your paper. Watch the video(s) and take notes.

2. Write a Draft

Reread the career profiles of Steve Hebert and Molly Dill, and look at the structure for ideas. Then write your paper. You might find it helpful to discuss the answer to one interview question in each paragraph. Also try to use direct quotes. They will make your paper more interesting.

Alternatively, you could record your interview and create a podcast. If you do this, make sure you have a clear recording without background noise so listeners can understand. You can also create comments about the interview and include them into your final product.

3. Get feedback.

Exchange papers with a partner, and read your partner's paper. You may not feel comfortable with editing, but you can tell your partner where you are confused. Also tell your partner about the parts you enjoy or want to learn more about.

4. Revise.

Read your paper and make improvements. Some writers find they say something twice in different words, so they need to cut unnecessary details. Other writers find they want to add new details when they revise. When you finish, your paragraphs should all be similar in size, and your sentences should not be too long. A combination of short and long sentences is usually effective.

5. Present

Present the information about your career profile in groups or to the whole class so people can learn about different careers. Ask and answer questions.

6. Edit

Edit your paper for mistakes and punctuation. Make final changes. Then turn in your final draft.

Sample Performance Day Schedule

Goal	Time	Activity
Warm-up	10 minutes	Cast assembles and sets up the stage.
Introduce Theme Critical thinking question	10 – 15 minutes	The director introduces a discussion topic – The critical thinking question of the play. The director invites students to do a pair-share about the following question. *Who decides what you study in college? You or your parents? How do you make that decision?*
Prepare audience	1 minute	Director introduces the play and asks people to turn off their cell phones.
Performance	20 minutes	Cast performs the play and takes a curtain call.
Post-Play Talkback	10 – 15 minutes	Director passes out paper for small groups to prepare questions for talkback. Director facilitates the talkback in which audience makes comments or asks the actors questions.

About the Author

ALICE SAVAGE comes from a family of theatre people. Her grandfather was a professor of theatre arts, and her father is a playwright. This family experience in the theatre combined with a love of teaching has given her opportunity to bring two passions together. In addition to *Her Own Worst Enemy*, Savage has also written a play called *Best Intentions*.

Currently, a professor of ESOL at Lone Star College System, in Houston, Texas, she is grateful for the opportunity to spend time with young people who are exploring their own decisions about career and life.

CPSIA information can be obtained
at www.ICGtesting.com
Printed in the USA
LVOW09s1051270318
571311LV00021B/311/P

9 781948 492034